# THANKSGIVING
## SCISSOR SKILLS
### WORKBOOK FOR PRESCHOOL

By MezzyArt Designs

FOR MORE VISIT US AT: **https://www.amazon.com/author/mezzyartdesigns**

All Rights Reserved © 2020

# THIS BOOK BELONGS TO:
..................................

Thank you for your purchase,
If you like the product, we would truly appreciate a short review on our Amazon product page.
Reviews are crucial for any author, and even just a line or two can make a huge difference.
Your opinion matters and is very much appreciated!

# THANKSGIVING CUTTING PRACTICE

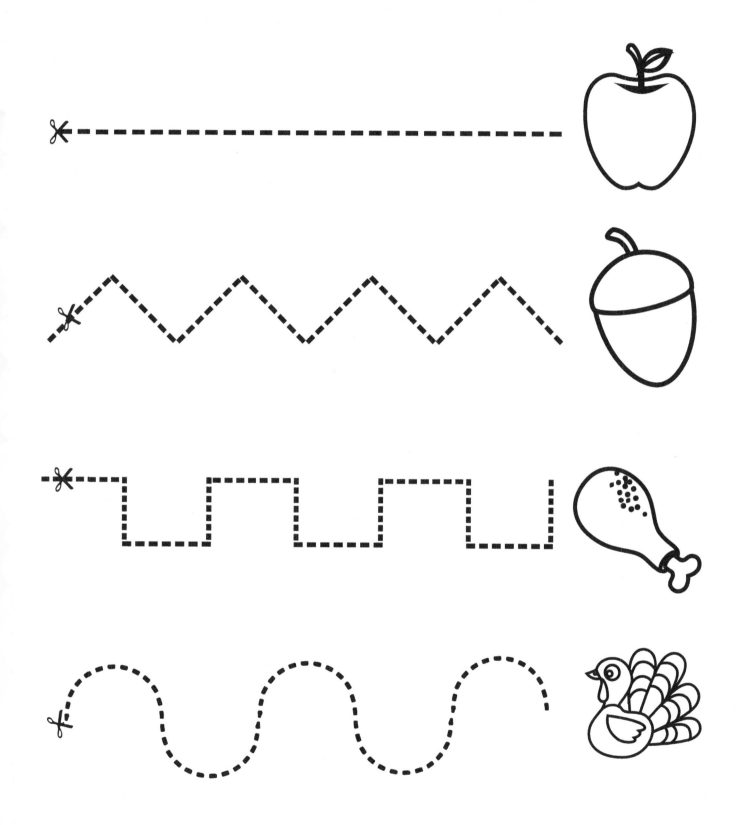

# Cut And Paste Thanksgiving Fun Faces!

# Cut And Paste Thanksgiving Fun Faces!

# Cut And Paste Thanksgiving Fun Faces!

# THANKSGIVING COUNTING
## Count, Cut and Paste the Right Number!

# THANKSGIVING COUNTING

Count, Cut and Paste the Right Number!

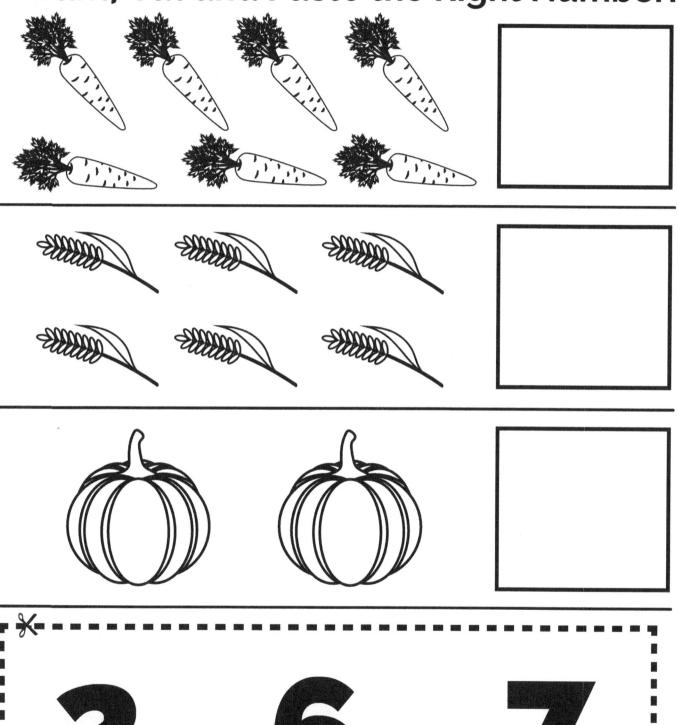

# What Picture Comes Next?

# What Picture Comes Next?

# Color, Cut and Paste the Apples in Order from 1 to 10.

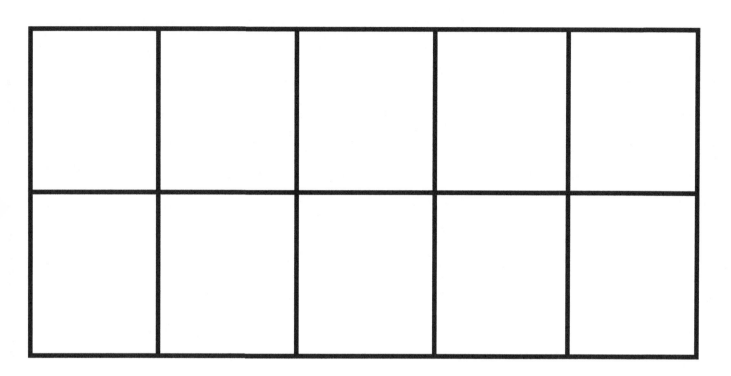

# THANKSGIVING SHADOW MATCH
## Cut and Paste pictures that match their shadows

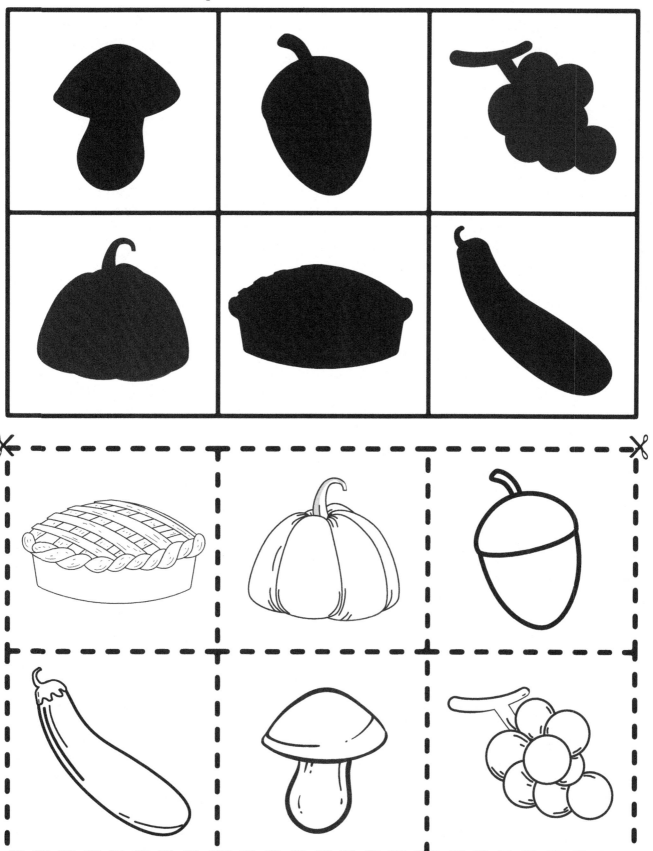

# THANKSGIVING SHADOW MATCH
## Cut and Paste pictures that match their shadows

# SMALLEST TO BIGGEST

Cut and Paste them in Order of smallest to biggest.

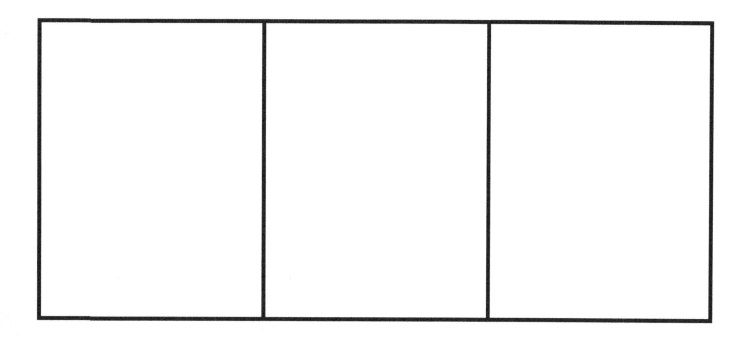

# BIGGEST TO SMALLEST

Cut and Paste them in Order of biggest to smallest.

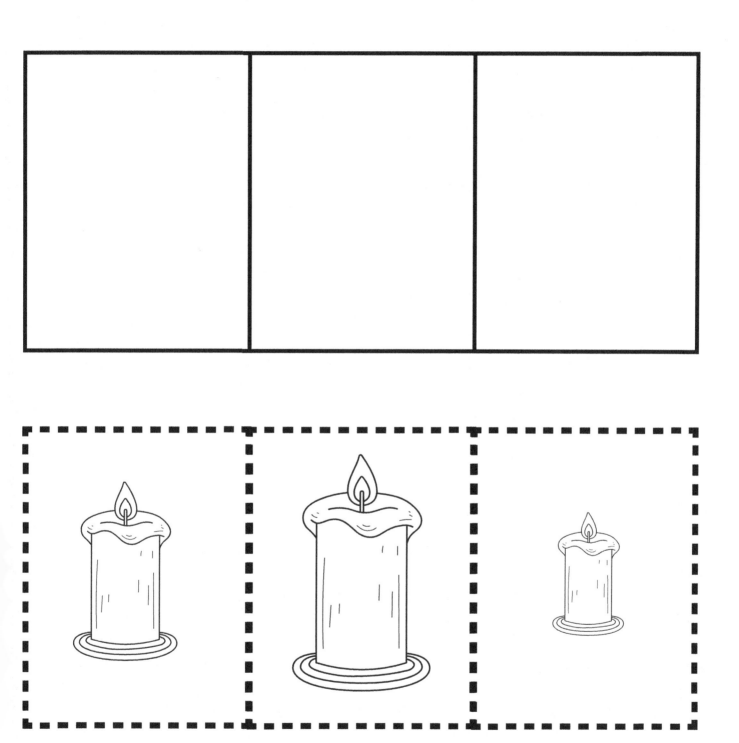

# Cut and Paste inside the Right Box!

# THANKSGIVING COLORING
## COLOR AND CUT!

# THANKSGIVING COLORING
## COLOR AND CUT!

# THANKSGIVING COLORING
## COLOR AND CUT!

# THANKSGIVING COLORING
## COLOR AND CUT!

# THANKSGIVING COLORING
## COLOR AND CUT!

# THANKSGIVING COLORING
## COLOR AND CUT!

# THANKSGIVING COLORING
## COLOR AND CUT!

# THANKSGIVING COLORING
## COLOR AND CUT!

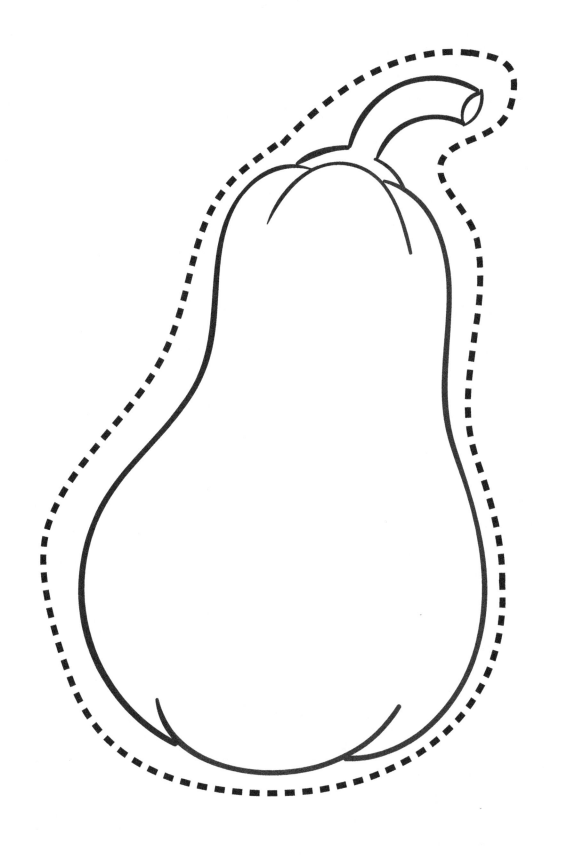

Made in the USA
Coppell, TX
16 November 2022

86476767R00031